The
Arena Book:
Central Europe

By Tyler Bilton

Copyright
The Arena Book: Central Europe
by Tyler Bilton

© Tyler Bilton 2018

ISBN 978-91-639-6015-4

Contents

Introduction

Jégcsarnok. Eishalle. Ledena dvorana. Zimní stadion. Ice arena.

No two hockey arenas are alike. Even the arenas that are built using the same blueprints will have different characteristics and develop their own chipped paint, puck marks, smells, and history.

A hockey arena is unique from any other sporting venue as they are designed to replicate winter indoors, because hockey was born on frozen ponds and lakes. Then, in Montreal on March 3, 1875, the game was moved indoors for the first time. Hockey is now being played in countries like the United Arab Emirates, Australia, Mexico, Brazil, and many others.

Arenas are a place for players to become artists. It is in the arena that they are able to showcase their craft, because hockey requires unique athletic dexterity and an harmonic balance of brute force and delicate grace.

My affinity for hockey arenas developed as soon as I could skate. Visiting the local arena was as magical to me as visiting an amusement park. The sound of pucks hitting the boards or glass, the lingering smell of popcorn from the big junior hockey game the night before, the exhaust from the Zamboni intertwined with frozen air, the sound of steel carving up the ice, and the way fog hangs just above the sheet waiting to be dispersed by the first player to step on the ice - it was and always will be a feast for my senses.

I have been able to travel extensively for hockey and, no matter what town I am in or going to visit, the first thing I look up is where the hockey arena is. Of course, there are times where I have to know where the arena is because I will be coaching or scouting. But, even on holidays, you will find me in an arena at some point. I have visited over 300

arenas so far and will visit every arena I possibly can.

This book is not only a passion, but it is my life. I feel it's important to understand the history that surrounds these facilities. We get caught up in getting to the rink, playing the game or watching the game then hurrying to leave, sometimes never appreciating these unique facilities. And in Europe, lots of these rinks have character and are unique to themselves. This collection of photos was taken between 2014 and 2016, during two seasons of coaching and scouting. Instead of describing the arenas, I wanted the photos to do just that, and I chose to discuss the history of the towns and hockey clubs where the arenas are located.

Please enjoy this book and the others hopefully to come. Even if we don't share the same love for hockey, I hope you will enjoy the beauty and history of these magnificent facilities.

Yours in hockey, Tyler Bilton

1.
Jihlava, Czech Republic

WC
←

3

Horácký Zimní Stadion
49°23′53″ N, 15°35′0″ E

The first reference to the settlement that became known as Jihlava was in 1233. 723 years later a hockey club arrived.

The walled city in the Bohemian-Moravian highlands became the heart of European mining in the 13th century. After wars, fires, and occupation by the Swedes, the city always managed to rebuild and reinvent itself. While under the Austria-Hungary Empire, Jihlava became a key textile producer, and a young boy named Gustav Mahler found his affinity for music that would lead him to Vienna and become a world renowned composer and conductor.

After World War I, the sporting culture grew in Jihlava. The first mention of ice hockey being organised was on December 16, 1929. In 1956, one of the most decorated hockey clubs in Czech hockey history was formed, HC Dukla Jihlava.

Horácký Zimní Stadion, Ice Hockey
Stadium, began construction in 1954 and
welcomed Dukla Jihlava in 1956. The club
arrived out of necessity as a place for
the military hockey team to live, train and
play.

The newly renovated practice arena has a smaller ice surface and used to be an outdoor rink. The main hall has a capacity of 7,500. The German name for the city is Iglau which comes from the word for hedgehog. That is why the hedgehog is featured in the city's coat of arms (and on Dukla's logo).

AUTO MÁCA
AUTOCENTRUM JIHLAVA
POZEMNÍ STAVBY Jihlava
Clea
BIONA
W|S|M

Success didn't arrive immediately, but under head coach Jaroslav Pitner the club began to peak in the 1960s. From 1967 to 1972, Dukla Jihlava were Czechoslovakian league champions. To date, the club has 12 top league championships, three second league championships, four Spengler Cup golds, and four silvers and four bronzes in the European Cup Championships.

After the Velvet Revolution and the fall of the Iron Curtain, funding for the army slowly ceased and players were able to search for professional contracts outside of the country. In 1999, the city took over control of Jihlava but the club was relegated to the second division. It made it back to the top in 2004-05 but was relegated. In 2017, the club earned promotion to the top league yet again.

Jaroslav Pitner led Dukla Jihlava from
1958 to 1982 — one of the longest
coaching tenures in hockey history.
Players like Jan Suchy, Bobby Holik, Jiri
Holik, Michal Rozsival, Michal Pivonka,
and Dominik Hasek once wore the
signature Dukla maroon and yellow
jersey.

To date, the club and city have over 20
players selected in the NHL Draft.

2.
Topoľčany, Slovakia

Topol'čany Zimný Štadión
48°33'37.2"N, 18°09'46.8"E

Settled on the Nitra River in western Slovakia — which flows south until it joins the Vah which then empties into the Danube — the area around Topol'čany has been settled since the Early Stone Age. Over the centuries, the area has seen a multitude of occupants come through the Nitra River valley and Topol'čany has seen its fair amount of hockey clubs call the town home.

Slav rulers built a castle nearby in the 9th century — the ruins can be still seen today — and the first recorded mention of Topol'čany was in 1173. Hungarian rule fell to Ottoman rule, in which most of the occupants that survived the destruction of the town were enslaved. The town came back under Hungarian rule when the Austrian empire joined with the Hungarian empire.

After World War I, a new Czech-Slovak state emerged. In 1932, a hockey club was formed in Topol'čany that began playing outdoors on a frozen football (soccer) field. The city had different clubs competing under a variety of names, but hockey began to flourish.

However, World War II broke out and Slovakia fell under the control of the Nazis. Liberated by Soviet and Romanian forces, Czechoslovakia fell under the wing of communism and hockey came back to Topol'čany with more clubs. In 1969, the first artificial ice arena was completed and it is still used today. A roof was built on top of the Topol'čany Zimný Štadión in 1972.

From 1978 to 1988, Topoľčany had a military hockey club that was affiliated with the legendary Slovak club, Dukla Trencin. They adopted the similar yellow and red jerseys of their parent club and the other Dukla, Dukla Jihlava.

The affiliation ended in 1988 with an independent military team being formed and competing until 1993. After Slovakia became an independent state, the military teams were eventually disbanded.

The two clubs that were competing in Topoľčany at the time, HC Topoľčany (civilian) and VTJ Topoľčany (military), joined together and have competed as one club ever since.

The arena in Topoľčany has a capacity of 3,400 and used to be named the Topvar Arena. Topvar is a top selling beer in Slovakia that used to be brewed in Topoľčany. Despite the loss of the brewery, Topoľčany has remained an important industrial town for furniture manufacturing and technologies.

Success has evaded HC Topoľčany
in its hockey life. The club has
primarily participated at the second tier
professional level in Czechoslovakia
and Slovakia with their most successful
season being in the 2004-05 season.
That season, they finished second in
the standings but lost in the finals to HC
Detva.

Despite the lack of trophies, the town has produced notable graduates to the NHL including Lubomir Visnovsky and Miroslav Satan. Six players have also been selected in the NHL Draft.

3.
Budapest, Hungary

23

Tüskecsarnok
47°28'18.12"N, 19°3'28.08"E

On the western side of the Danube River, in Budapest's District XI, is a limestone memorial created by Hungarian artist Péterfy László. The memorial has two identical columns atop a small flight of stairs with faces carved into the limestone. Cold and anonymous, the faces hover above in an unforgettable chilling gaze that humbles one when standing in the middle. The memorial is dedicated to the victims murdered by the communist regime between 1945-1956 — a reminder of just one of the many incidents that have shaped Hungary. A short walk away from Egyetemisták Park, where the memorial sits, is one of Budapest's newly minted sporting arenas called Tüskecsarnok or 'Spiked Hall' in English.

There are many monuments and memorials in Budapest. The city has accumulated lots of scars after centuries of wars, occupations, and revolutions but remains one of the jewels of Europe. Like other cities, Budapest found its life from the Danube River as Celts settled first before the Romans came in and named it Aquincum.

Budapest is actually a combination of three cities that officially merged in 1873. Prior to the merger Buda and Obuda, on the west, and Pest, on the east, were separate. Buda became the capital of Hungary in 1361.

Both World Wars impacted Budapest and Hungary, but World War II left the city in ruins with hundreds of thousands dead. In 1941, Hungary joined Nazi Germany to invade the Soviet Union. However, Hungary tried to leave the pact after. The Nazis invaded Hungary and installed a puppet government starting a dark period in Hungary, especially in Budapest.

The Battle of Budapest lasted from December 1944 to February 1945 and concluded with the Soviet Union defeating the Nazi's and taking control of Hungary.

On October 23, 1956, a violent uprising took place in Budapest to overthrow the Soviet rulers. The bloody and violent revolution lasted into November but was won by the Soviet army. The date of the start of the revolution is now a national holiday and not only remembers the 1956 Revolution, but also the eventual formation of the Hungarian Third Republic in 1989.

In the early 1990's, Tüskecsarnok started being built with the intention of it being used for the 1995 World Expo. Tüskecsarnok was near completion when construction was abandoned after Hungary withdrew from hosting the World Expo with Austria.

In 2012, renovations began to take
place on Tüskecsarnok. By 2014, a
massive sporting complex arose, with
Tüskecsarnok being the heart of it.

The spiked roof arena seats 2,540 and is now home to Magyar Atlétikai Club (MAC) Budapest men's and U20 teams. MAC Budapest competes in the professional Erste Liga (formerly the MOL Liga) that has teams in Hungary, Romania, and in 2016 welcomed a club from Serbia.

The arena and complex are also home
to Kanadai Magyar Hokiklub (KMH)
Budapest. KMH's men's team plays its
home games in Tüskecsarnok (in the
Slovakian 3rd tier league) while the youth
teams play in a tented arena next door.

An academy, MAC Budapest, started in the early 1960's and its youth teams are located in a Soviet-era outdoor stadium called Kisstadion - located next to the historic Ferenc Puskás Stadium. A circus-like tent has been installed over the ice at Kisstadion so they can play without weather interruptions.

The Hungarian men's national hockey team made its debut in 1927 and their first Olympic appearance in 1928 in St.Moritz, Switzerland. In St.Moritz, they finished last losing to Great Britain, France, and Belgium. Canada, coached by Conn Smythe, won gold. Ten years later at the World Championships in Prague, Hungary tied Canada 1-1 and finished seventh in the standings (tied with USA and Poland).

The MAC Budapest men's team is young to the Erste Liga, but made it to the finals in 2015-16 and 2016-17 season. Both times they lost to Hungarian club, DVTK Jegesmedvék Miskolc. However, MAC defeated Miskolc to capture the 2017 Hungarian Cup and bringing it back to Budapest for the first time since 1995.

Hungary's national men's team returned
to the IIHF World Championships in 2016
and had their first win in 77 years. The
women's national team and men's U20
national team were promoted from their
groups in 2016.

In 2017, Tüskecsarnok hosted the Under-18 Women's Division 1 Group A championship — hockey is growing again in Hungary.

4.
Znojmo,
Czech Republic

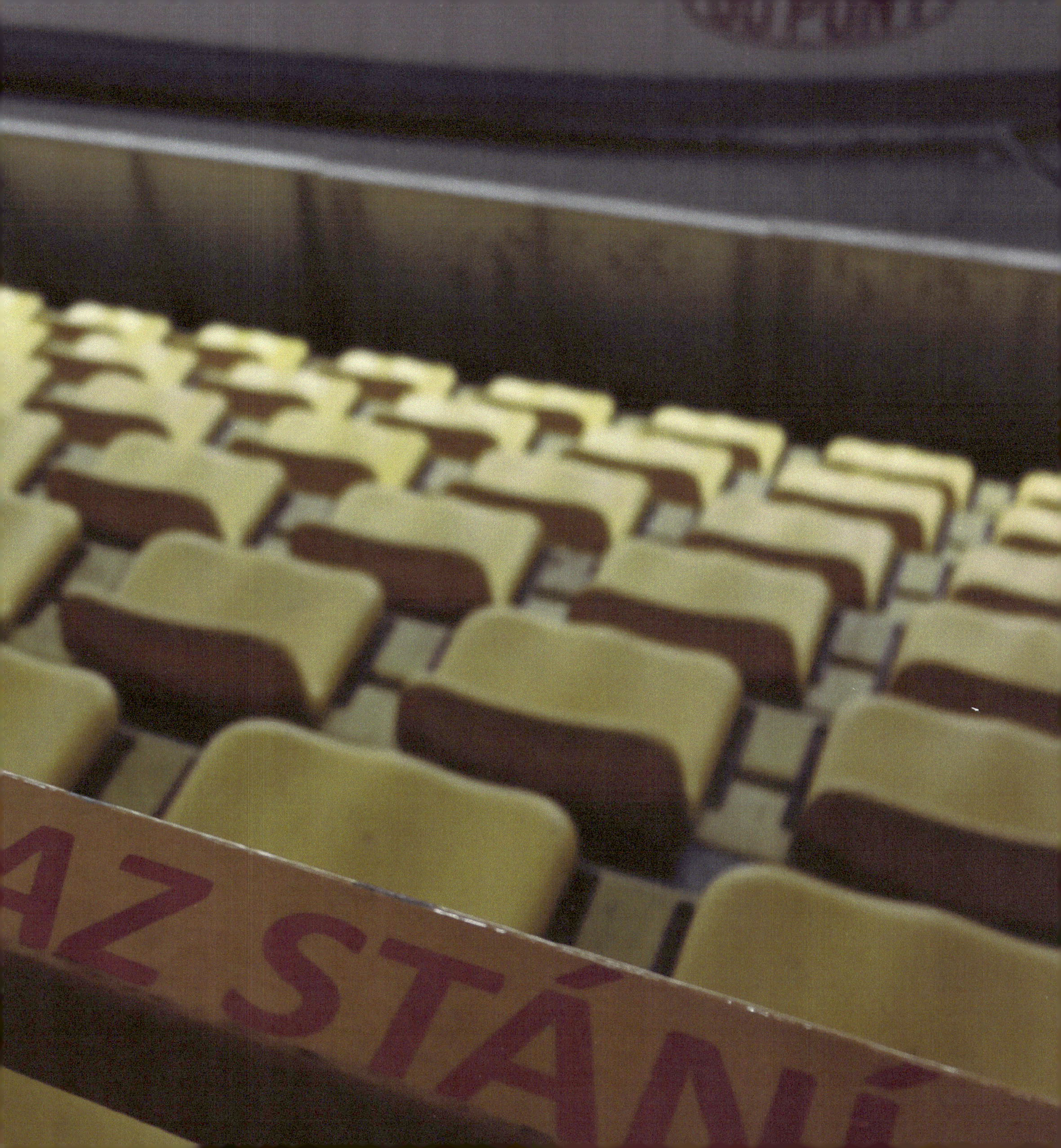

AZ STÁNÍ

Zimní Stadion Znojmo
48°51'37"N, 16°2'37"E

In the southern part of the Czech Republic, on the Austrian border, is the smallest National Park in the country. Winding along the Dyje River, Podyjí National Park starts in the west near Vranov nad Dyjí and finishes in the east by Znojmo. The park holds incredible panoramas, old castle ruins, stone bridges over 2000 years old, World War II pillboxes, and has a section of the Iron Curtain - the last preserved piece in the country.

A phrase famously coined by Winston Churchill, the Iron Curtain divided Europe after World War II — both literally and ideologically. Behind the Iron Curtain were countries under the Soviet Union sphere. On the surface, the intention behind the barrier was to keep out the West and its influences. But in truth, the Iron Curtain became a wall of a prison, and trying to escape from it was risking your life and the lives of those you knew.

After the Velvet Revolution in 1989 and the fall of Soviet influence, the Iron Curtain became irrelevant as borders opened up.

About 17km away from this piece of history is the ancient fortified city of Znojmo. An important trade route, and known for its wine, Znojmo's earliest mention was in the 9th century. During the 14th and 15th centuries, construction of Znojmo's underground passageways began. The passageways, which can still be toured today, were used as an extension of the city's fortification as well as a way to store and transport goods.

Like many cities in Europe, war shaped Znojmo due to its position on an important trade route between Prague and Vienna. The Swedes looted the city during the Thirty-Years War and in 1742 the Prussians invaded. On his way to his famous Battle of Austerlitz, Napoleon stayed in Znojmo and returned in 1809 for the Battle of Znaim (German for Znojmo).

In 1933, a hockey club formed called TJ Znojmo. World War II put a hold on hockey's development but in 1970 the Zimní Stadion Znojmo was built, beginning a new era for hockey in Znojmo.

Besides the barbed wire, sometimes triple-layers of fencing, guard towers and armed soldiers with dogs, the Iron Curtain was also electrified.

With a capacity of 4,800, the arena was renamed Hostan Arena in 2004, after a sponsorship with Hostan beer. In 2016, the arena was again renamed and will now be called Nevoga Arena for the next four years.

Since the club's inception, it has had a few different names: TJ Sokol Znojmo; Sk Agropodnik Znojmo; HC Excalibur Znojemští Orli; HC JME Znojemští Orli; HC Znojemští Orli, and now Orli Znojmo.

The club earned promotion to the top Czech Extraliga in 1999, after defeating Dukla Jihlava in a best-of-seven series. After ten seasons in the top league, the club started to struggle financially and sold its Extraliga license to Brno in 2009.

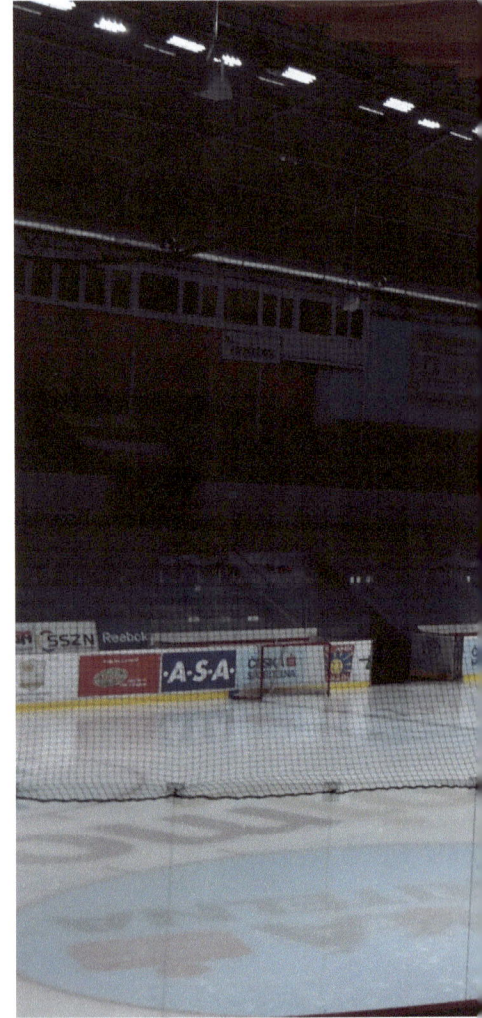

In 2011, Orli Znojmo made the decision
to be the first Czech club to leave
the country and join the Erste Bank
Eishockey Liga. Based out of Austria and
also featuring clubs in Croatia, Hungary,
Italy, and Slovenia, the EBEL does not
have promotion and relegation.

During the 2004-05 NHL lockout, Patrik Elias, Martin Havlat and Tomas Vokoun joined Znojmo, while Bryan Bickell suited up during the 2012-13 NHL lockout. Czech Hockey Hall of Fame members Jiri Dopita and Karel Rachunek also once wore the Orli Znojmo jersey.

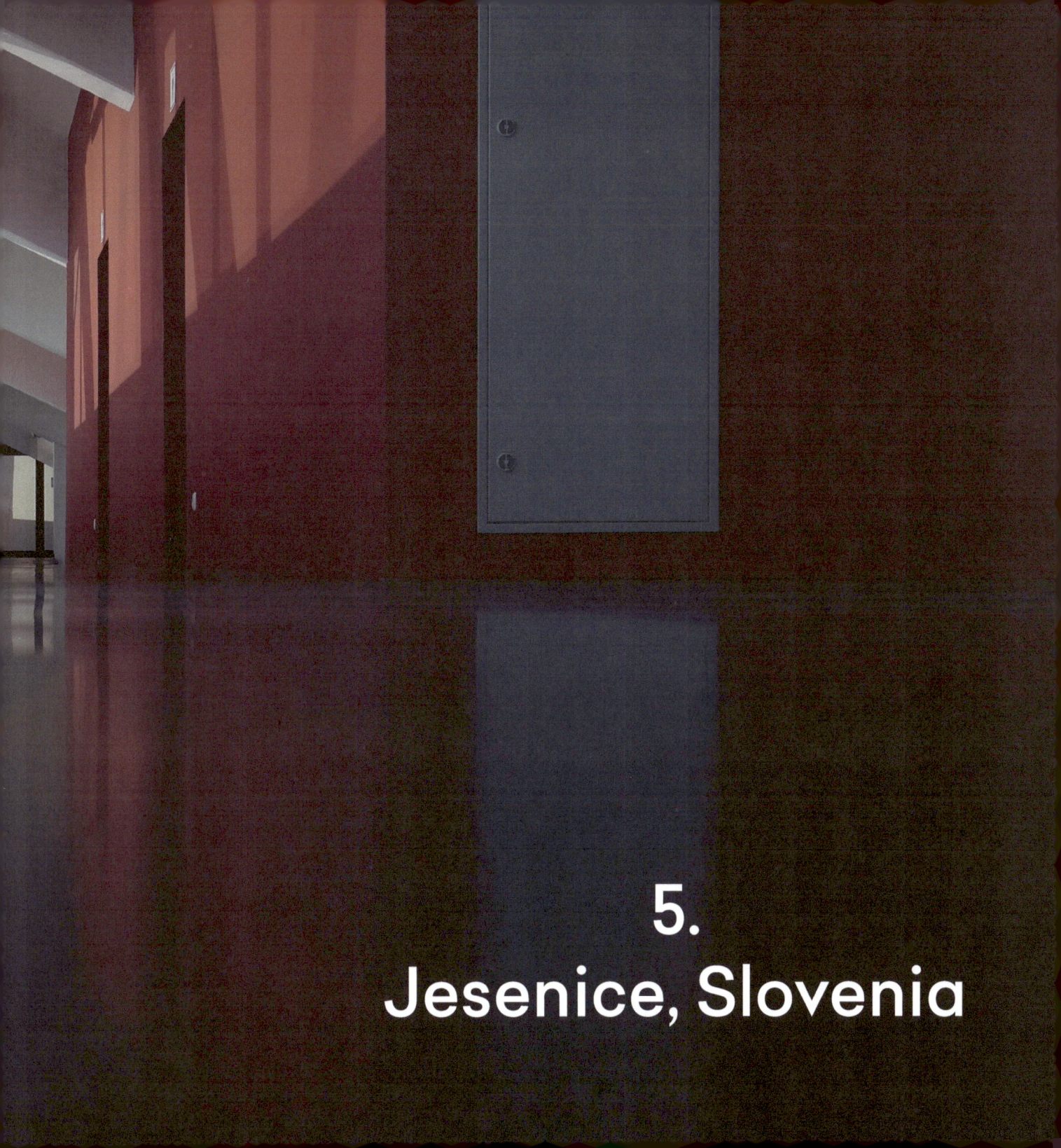

5.
Jesenice, Slovenia

Dvorana Podmežakla
46° 25'59.04"N, 14°3'1.12"E

The quickest way to Jesenice from western Europe is going through the Karawanken mountain range. Rising above 2,200m, it forms a natural border between Austria and Slovenia. The Karawanken Tunnel is 7,864m long and depending on the speed limit and traffic volume can give passengers the impression they will arrive in Africa instead of Slovenia when travelling through it.

After the opening of the tunnel on June 1, 1991, it was captured by the Yugoslav Army at the onset of the Slovenian War that started on June 26. Slovenia had been a part of Yugoslavia but declared its independence on June 25, which caused the Yugoslav army to mobilise. Fighting broke out in scattered areas around the country but after ten days a ceasefire was agreed and the Brioni Accord was signed, which eventually lead to Slovenia gaining its independence. While the fighting stopped in Slovenia, trouble was brewing in the rest of Yugoslavia and another war was about to break out, with the aftershocks still felt today.

Jesenice is known for its steel industry, nature and hockey. The steel industry has shaped the city since the early 14th century and Jesenice boasts that its product can be found in the Eiffel Tower, Cern Reactor and Titanic. But its factories were coveted by others during periods of war and the city was captured in both World Wars.

The Sava River flows through Jesenice, Slovenia, Croatia and eventually connects with the Danube in Belgrade. Surrounding the Sava River are the Karawanken Mountains and the Mežakla plateau. Mežakla is part of the Julian Alps — named after Julius Caesar — and the Triglav National Park. Triglav is the highest peak in Slovenia and is featured on the country's flag, coat of arms, and sometimes the national team's hockey jersey.

In Mežakla's shadow is the Dvorana Podmežakla. Built in 1978, it became a home for Yugoslavia and Slovenia's most decorated hockey club as well as one of its most famous players, Anze Kopitar.

Hockey was played on the frozen football fields that are now next door to Dvorana Podmežakla before Jesenice constructed the first artificial ice arena in Yugoslavia in 1954. Dvorana Podmežakla replaced the old arena in 1978 and underwent massive renovations in 2011 and 2013. It now holds 4,500 fans for hockey and 5,500 for basketball.

Steel and hockey have almost been synonymous in Jesenice. The steel mill, Acroni, gave its name to a club that would become HK Acroni Jesenice in 1948. With a thriving industry, Acroni Jesenice thrived as well, winning 23 Yugoslav national championships.

After Slovenia became independent, Acroni Jesenice continued to dominate Slovenian hockey, winning nine Slovenian national championships. In 2006, the team decided to join the higher level Austrian-based Erste Bank Eishockey Liga (EBEL), despite financial difficulties occurring in 1999.

Dvorana Podmežakla was the site of the Stanley Cup being raised by Jesenice's own Anze Kopitar in 2012. But the high from that party was erased soon after, as Acroni Jesenice was folded due to bankruptcy. After mounting a 2.5 million Euro debt, the club was kicked out of the EBEL and it appeared the hockey glory days had passed.

A new club, HDD Jesenice emerged soon after the collapse of Acorni Jesenice and joined the new Inter-National League (INL) that featured Austrian and Slovenian clubs.

In the summer of 2014, the arena
welcomed back Kopitar and the Stanley
Cup, and a few months later HDD
Jesenice won the Slovenian national
championship.

A new second tier professional league, based in Austria, was formed in the 2016-17 season called the Alps Hockey League (AlpsHL). The new league includes eight teams from Italy, seven from Austria, and HDD Jesenice. In 2017, Jesenice won another Slovenian National Championship defeating EBEL club, Olimpija Ljubljana.

6.
Miskolc, Hungary

HAZAI PÁLYÁN
BORSODI
OLC
ŠKODA
Zenit-Auto Rent
FLOTTAKEZELÉS, AUTÓKÖLCSÖNZÉS
MISKOLC HOLDING
Auchan
SZINVAPARK
Piano
ÉMÁSZ

Miksolci Jégcsarnok
48°5'46"N, 20°47'17"E

Like most ancient cities, Miskolc was established on a location that provided natural resources and access to trading. Miskolc and its surrounding area boast a history that dates back to prehistoric times. Its location in a river valley on key trading routes made it an ideal location for many historic tribes to settle there. The discovery of iron ore fields increased its importance.

One of the best ways of determining the history of an area is the excavation of cemeteries and burial mounds. Remnants of Scythians and Sarmatian tribes (Iranian nomads) have been found in the area. After came the Celts that settled in 350 BCE and left behind 367 Celtic coins that were discovered in 1846. Next came the Romans and Germanic tribes. Bronze jewels and iron tools were discovered in a cemetery, giving evidence that the Avars settled in the area between the 7th and 8th centuries.

The 20th century brought factories, heavy industry and a sporting culture to Miskolc. On February 6, 1910, the football club Diósgyőr-Vasgyári Testgyakorlók Köre (Diósgyőr Iron Factory-Test Practitioners Circle) or DVTK, was founded. Organised hockey made its appearance in Miskolc sixty-eight years later. The first hockey arena opened in 1978 and the Miskolci Kinizsi hockey club was started.

Mindszenti temető (All Saints Cemetery) is one of the current cemeteries in Miskolc. The cemetery is the final resting place for some notable residents and shares a parking lot with the Miksolci Jégcsarnok (Miskolc Ice Hall) that was opened in 2006. The new 1,804 (1,304 seating) capacity arena was the first step in creating a new Hungarian hockey dynasty.

As the industrial boom began to fade in Miskolc, Miskolci Kinizsi ran into financial difficulties. The club ceased operations in 1990 but fortunately a new club was formed before the 1990-1991 season started. The club ran into trouble again and in 1994 a new organisation was formed, Miskolci Jegesmedvék JSE (Miskolc Polar Bears JSE). The Polar Bears found a stable ground and began to grow.

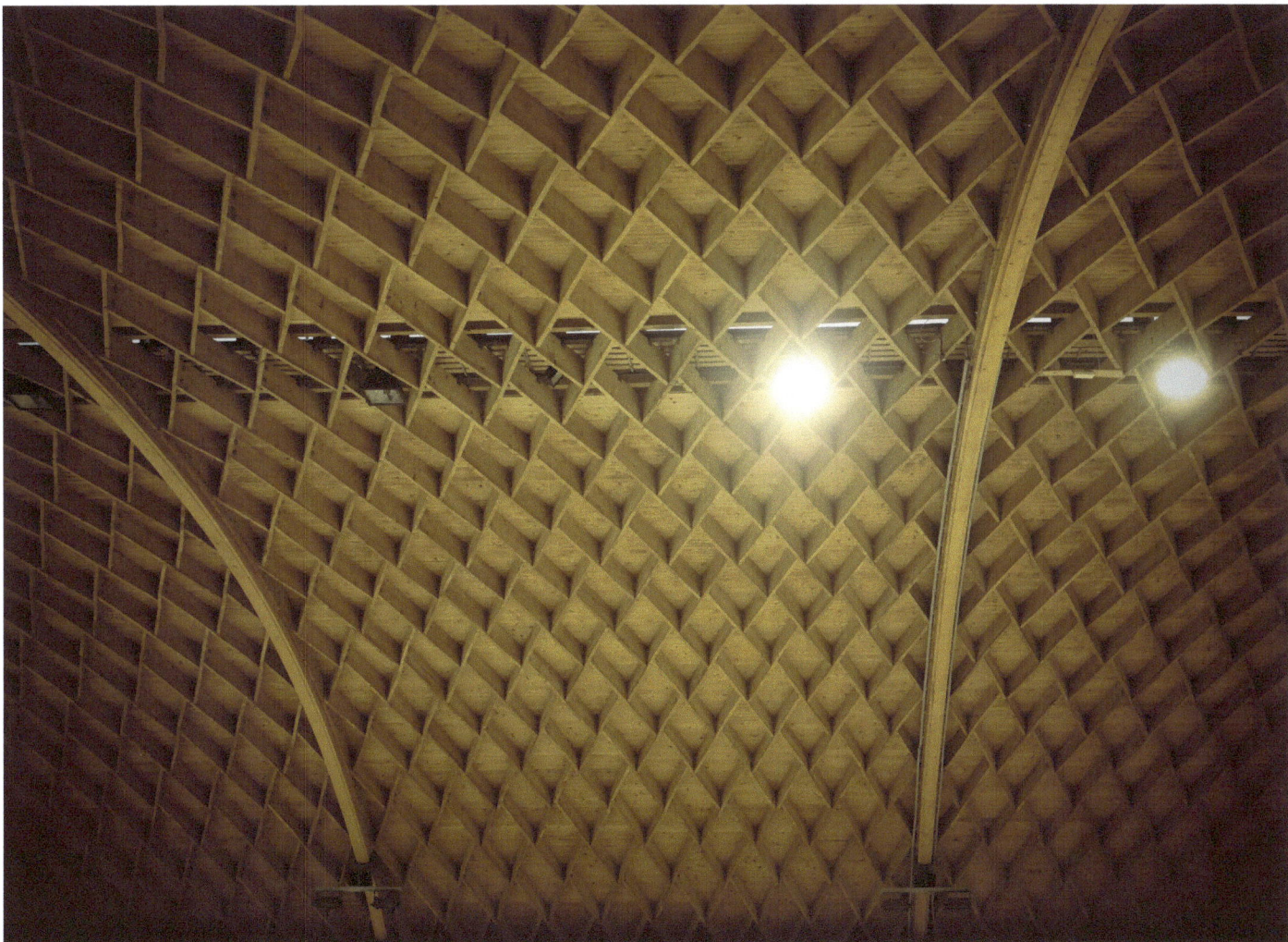

The Polar Bears development was aided by the new Miksolci Jégcsarnok that opened in 2006. In 2008, they joined the new Hungarian based Erste Liga (formerly MOL Liga) along with four teams from Romania and five from Hungary. Out of 36 games, Miskolc only won three games and finished second last.

The 2011-12 season brought the Polar Bears their first taste of championship hockey. After finishing fourth in the league, they made it to the finals but lost to Hungarian club Dunaújváros AC. Slovakian club HK Nove Zamky joined the Erste Liga in the 2012-13 season becoming champions in 2014 - the first time the league was won by a club outside of Hungary and Romania.

HK Nove Zamky's reign didn't last long; The Polar Bears won their first Erste Liga championship in 2015 sweeping HK Nove Zamky in the best-of-seven series. Game one of the series wasn't even played due to a scheduling conflict for HK Nove Zamky - they were competing in Slovakia's third-tier professional league playoffs at the same time. So the Polar Bears won 5-0 by default.

In game four, the Polar Bears were losing 4-0 but won in overtime 5-4 thanks to a hat-trick - including the game winner - from Columbus Blue Jackets draft pick Jesse Dudas.

BÉRLETES HELY

JEGESMEDVÉK

29

Before the 2015-16 season started, the
Polar Bears saw another organisational
change by moving under the DVTK
umbrella. Besides football, DVTK has
basketball, table tennis, wrestling, and
chess clubs.

Rebranded as DVTK Jegesmedvék and changing their colours from yellow and black to red and white, the club continued their winning ways, capturing the 2016 Erste Liga championship sweeping MAC Budapest. For the 2017-18, the club also released a new logo.

In 2017, the DVTK Polar Bears became the first team in Erste Liga history to not only win three championships but also win them in a row. They again defeated MAC Budapest in the series 4-1.

7.
Prague, Czech Republic

arena

Sportovní Hala
50°6'25" N, 14°26'0" E

In 1893, an athletic club was formed in Prague and started playing football. By 1903, a bandy club started and in 1909 made a switch to ice hockey. The club became well known for the large 'S' it wore on the front of their uniforms which stood for Sparta. Over the decades, the club went through multiple name changes but one word that always remained was Sparta. The club grew up during defining moments in not only Prague's but Europe's history.

Prague - or Praha in Czech - continues to be one of Europe's most popular cities. The city's physical beauty lies in the buildings and structures showcasing the different styles of architecture that swept through the city over the centuries.

The region has been settled since 5000 BCE and the site that is now Prague can be traced back to the 9th century. The Bohemian capital flourished in the 14th century with help of Charles IV. The Holy Roman Emperor started a development phase and one of his projects included the formation of Charles University in 1348. The first university in central Europe, it has attracted many notable academics including Jan Hus, Tycho Brahe, Johannes Kepler, and Albert Einstein.

The Reformation and Thirty Years War had Prague as the backdrop. The Swedes sacked Prague in 1648 and took with them the ancient manuscript, Codex Gigas - which still resides in Stockholm's library.

In 1848, revolts against the ruling Austrian Habsburgs began to flare up all over the empire, including in Prague. But it wasn't until the end of World War I that the empire dissolved and Prague became the capital of the new republic, Czechoslovakia.

The Nazis took control during World War II until Czechoslovakia was liberated in 1945 and became a part of the Soviet Union sphere after a coup d'état by the Communist Party. Despite the conditions, hockey began to grow behind the iron curtain and the Czechoslovakian national team (CSSR) became a powerful contender on the international stage. In 1947, the CSSR team won their first IIHF World Championship in Prague, defeating the Swedes. The game was played in the outdoor arena, Zimní stadion Štvanice.

The world's largest monument to Josef Stalin was unveiled in 1955 by the Czechoslovakian Communist Party. That same year the first hockey match was televised in the country from Zimní stadion Štvanice. The 50 metre high stone and marble statue towered over Prague, but Moscow ordered it taken down and thus it was blown up in 1962 - the same year Sparta Prague's brand new 13,238 capacity arena opened, the Sportovní Hala (Sports Hall).

In the spring of 1968, the Czechoslovakian Communist Party attempted to reform the structure of communism which became known as the "Prague Spring." The Warsaw Pact countries - led by the Soviet Union - invaded Czechoslovakia to overthrow the movement. The 1969 IIHF World Championship was supposed to be hosted by Czechoslovakia but, with the invasion, the tournament was moved to Stockholm. By chance, the CSSR team met the Soviets not once but twice in the tournament. Charged by the situation back home, the CSSR team defeated the Soviets in both games. Until that moment, the Soviets had never been defeated twice in one tournament by the same opponent. Despite that, the Soviets still won gold and CSSR took away the bronze. One of the most well-known Czech hockey players, Jaromir Jagr, wears the number 68 to commemorate the Prague Spring, despite being born in 1972.

The Velvet Revolution began in Prague in 1989 and led to the end of one-party rule in Czechoslovakia. 1992 was the last time the CSSR competed at the World Championships, defeating Switzerland for the bronze medal at the Sportovní Hala. By 1993, Czechoslovakia split, creating the Czech Republic and Slovakia. The Czech Republic won their first medal, a bronze, at the 1993 World Championships. Slovakia wouldn't earn their first medal until the 2000 World Championships in Russia - a silver, after losing to the Czech Republic.

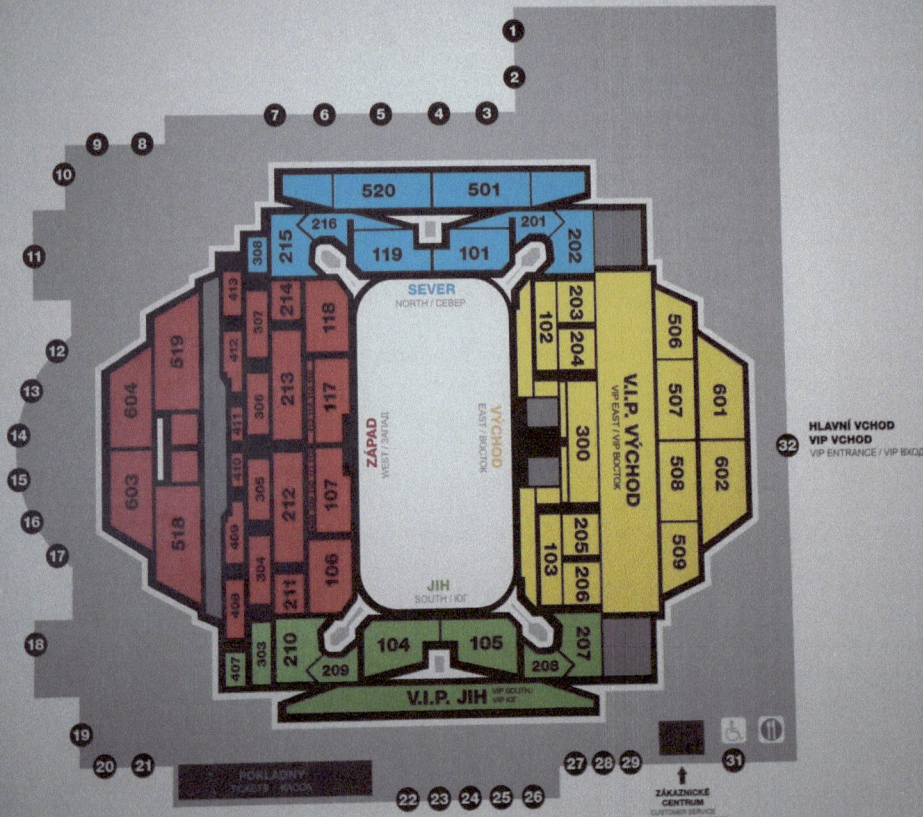

NÁVŠTĚVNÍ ŘÁD A PLÁN ARENY
ПРАВИЛА ПОСЕЩЕН И АРЕНОЙ ПЛАН / RULES FOR VISITORS AND SEATING PLAN

Tipsport

Over the years, the Sportovní Hala has had a few different names. From 1999 to 2002 it was the Paegas Arena; from 2002 to 2008, T-Mobile Arena; from 2008 to 2011, Tesla Arena; and finally it is now called the Tipsport Arena. Regardless of the name, the Sportovní Hala will always hold a special place for Czechoslovakian, Czech, and Sparta Prague members and fans.

Like the arena, Sparta Prague has had some name changes over the years: AC Sparta Praha; Sokol Sparta Bubeneč; ZSJ Bratrství Sparta Praha; ZSJ Sparta ČKD Sokolovo Praha; TJ Spartak Praha Sokolovo and TJ Sparta ČKD Praha. But the club will always simply be Sparta. KHL club, HC Lev Praha also called the Sportovní Hala home from 2012-14.

HC Sparta Prague celebrated their 110th anniversary in the 2013-14 season by finishing atop the Czech Extraliga with 110 points. While the club hasn't won the most championships in top flight hockey, it remains one of the legendary franchises in Europe for its longevity.

A charter member of the Czechoslovakian top league in 1936, Sparta have won eight league championships - 1953, 1954, 1990, 1993, 2000, 2002, 2006, and 2007. They also won Spengler Cups in 1962 and 1963. The 2016-17 season saw the club reach the Champions Hockey League final for the first time, but they lost to Swedish club Frölunda HC.

Before the CSSR team boarded their plane destined for London to compete in the 1950 IIHF World Championship, the defending world champions were arrested - the entire team. They were charged with suspicion to defect by the Czechoslovak state security police (KNB). After a trial, 12 players were given prison terms with some being sent to labour camps.

The CSSR wouldn't win another world championship until 1972, knocking over the Soviets reign of consecutive championships from 1963 to 1971. The 1972 World Championship was held at the Sportovní Hala. The CSSR team also earned silver in 1978 and gold in 1985 at the Sportovní Hala. Not only used for hockey, the Czechoslovakian tennis team won the Davis Cup here 1980.

Sparta has had many well-known hockey names play for or coach the club. Some have NHL ties like Frantisek Kucera, Jan Hlavac, Jiri Hrdina, and David Volek but many are legends to Sparta and Czech hockey like Jiri Holecek, Pavel Richter, Vladimir Zabrodsky, Josef Malecek, Frantisek Tikal, Karel Gut and many more. Malecek famously turned down an offer from the New York Rangers in 1931.

In 2011, the New York Rangers played an exhibition game against Sparta Prague at the Sportovní Hala as part of the NHL's Premier Challenge. Four years later, Sparta officially relocated the new O2 Arena for all their home games. Sparta still uses the Hall for practices and their youth teams and the city still uses it for concerts and events.

Acknowledgements

Design and Layout
Travis Bilton

Editing
Victoria Heslop

Photographs and Information
Thank you to everyone I spoke to that gave permission to use my photos in this book. Thank you to those who offered their insight into the accuracy of the information in this book. In no particular order, thanks to: Emese Péter, Adam Nagy, Lukáš Peroutka, Valentina Gorišek, Tereza Velilovská, Ervin Mik, and Tereza Ščerbanová.

Special Thanks
Elias Vorlicek, thank you for giving me the opportunity to pursue my dream of coaching hockey in Europe. Your wisdom, hockey stories, and dinner parties will always be appreciated.

About the Author

Tyler Bilton has had many job titles in his life, but the ones he enjoys the most have 'hockey' in them. He was born on Vancouver Island, Canada, grew up in Penticton and has lived in five Canadian provinces, four US states, Turkey, Austria, and now resides outside Stockholm in Sweden. Tyler has a Bachelor of Science degree from Saint Michael's College and earned a Master of Arts degree from the University of Maine where his thesis examined the construction of gender identity through ice hockey.

Bibliography

Jihlava, Czech Republic
Bert van der Waal van Dijk (June 30, 2017) City of Jihlava (Iglau), Available at: http:// www.gustav-mahler.eu/index.php/ plaatsen/184-czech-republic/jihlava-iglau/995-city (Accessed: June 30, 2017).

EliteProspects.com () HC Dukla Jihlava, Available at: http://www. eliteprospects.com/team.php?team=1163 (Accessed: March 25, 2017).

HC Dukla Jihlava () History, Available at: http://www.hcdukla.cz/ zobraz.asp?t=historie (Accessed: February 10, 2017).

Lukáš Varhaník (2012) Lexicon of personalities of the hockey club HC Dukla Jihlava (Bachelor theses), Translated from Czech to English, České Budějovice: University of South Bohemia.

The Editors of Encyclopædia Britannica (September 02, 2011) Jihlava, Available at: https://www.britannica.com/place/Jihlava(- Accessed: March 7, 2017).

Tourist Information Centre Jihlava (May 20, 2008) History: Jihlava , Available at: https://www.jihlava.cz/en/vismo/dokumenty2. asp?id_org=100405&id=1001&p1=2680 (Accessed: February 10, 2017).

Topolcany, Slovakia
EliteProspects.com, HC Topolcany , Available at: http://www. eliteprospects.com/ team.php?team=1205 (Accessed: March 25, 2017).

IIHF.com (2008) Story #22: Bondra's Bomb - The biggest thing for Slovakia since independence , Available at: http://www.iihf. com/iihf-home/the-iihf/100-yearanniversary/ 100-top-stories/story-22/ (Accessed: April 17, 2017).

PrvaLiga.sk, HC Topoľč any, Available at: http://prvaliga.sk/ klub-topolcany (Accessed: March 27, 2017).

Robert Auty, Miroslav Blazek and Others (May 5, 2016) Slovakia, Available at: https:// www.britannica.com/place/Slovakia/History (Accessed: March 27, 2017).

The Editors of Encyclopaedia Britannica (March 28, 2017) Czechoslovakia, Available at: https://www.britannica.com/place/ Czechoslovakia (Accessed: March 28, 2017).

Veronika Ondrušová (November 20, 2015) History of the city (translated from Slovak to English), Available at: http://navstevnik. topolcany.sk/historia-mesta.phtml?id3=107337 (Accessed: October 1, 2016).

Vlastivedný slovník obcí na Slovensku, 3. časť, Topoľč any - History (translated from Slovak to English), Available at: https:// www.e-obce.sk/obec/topolcany/2-historia.html (Accessed: October 1, 2016).

Budapest, Hungary
Bohlen, Celestine (January 22, 1991) Budapest Gets Cold Feet On Big Fair With Vienna, Available at: http://www.nytimes. com/1991/01/22/world/budapest-gets-cold-feet-onbig-fair-with-vienna.html (Accessed: March 9, 2017).

Comite Olympique Suisse, 1928 Olympics Results, Available at: http://library.la84.org/6oic/OfficialReports/1928/1928w2 pdf (Accessed: March 5, 2017).

Communities of Hungarian Political Prisoners 1945-56 (June 30 , 1998) The inauguration of the MEMENTO 1945-1956 Monument (translated from Hungarian to English), Available at: http://mpek. hu/1998/06/a-memento-1945-1956-emlekmu-felavatasa/ (Accessed: March 10, 2017).

EliteProspects.com, MAC Budapest, Available at: http://www. eliteprospects.com/ team.php?team=19101 (Accessed: April 17, 2017).

EliteProspects.com, KMH Budapest, Available at: http://www. eliteprospects.com/team.php?team=21919 (Accessed: April 17, 2017).

Gabriel, Astrik L. and C. A. MacArtney (Edinburgh University Press 1966) Hungary: A Short History . [Online]. Available at: http://mek.oszk.hu/02000/02086/02086.htm (Accessed: March 9, 2017).

IceHockey.hu (November 17, 2013) Giant step for hockey in Budapest, Available at: http://en.icehockey.hu/hirek/hir/giant_step_ for_hockey_in_budapest(Accessed: March 9, 2017).

MACBudapesthockey.hu, About Us (translated from Hungarian to English), Available at: http://macbudapesthockey.hu/a-csapat/ (Accessed: June 2, 2017).

O'neil, Patrick H (1996) 'Revolution from within: Institutional analysis, transitions from authoritarianism, and the case of Hungary',

World Politics, (38), pp. 579-603.

Péter, László (May 18, 2017) Budapest, Available at: https://www.britannica.com/place/Budapest (Accessed: May 20, 2017).

Tamas, Koncz (August 15, 2014) Megvan a Tüskecsarnok befejezésének dátuma (translated from Hungarian to English), Available at: http://www.origo.hu/itthon/20140811-keso-osszel-nyithat-meg-a-tuskecsarnok.html (Accessed: March 9, 2017).

Tejfalussy, Béla, Hungarian Ice Hockey Association - History, Available at: http://www.icehockey.hu/oldalak/mjsz/toertenelem2(- Accessed: March 10, 2017).

The Editors of Encyclopaedia Britannica (March 27, 2017) Hungary, Available at: https:// www.britannica.com/place/Hungary/ (Accessed: March 27, 2017).

The Holocaust Explained, Case Study: Hungary , Available at: http://www.theholocaustexplained.org/ks3/life-in-nazi-occupied-europe/jews-in-occupiedcountries/hungary/#.WaVa23cjFsO (Accessed: March 10, 2017).

Zavodszky, Szabolcs (March 24, 2017) DVTK Jegesmedvek on top, Available at: http://www.iihf.com/home-of-hockey/news/news-singleview/?txttnews%5Btt_n%5D=11496&-cHash=e04798638570418898d4de282ad43db1 (Accessed: March 24, 2017).

Znojmo, Czech Republic
EliteProspects.com, Orli Znojmo, Available at: http://www.elite-prospects.com/team.php?team=9882 (Accessed: April 2, 2017).

HCOrli.cz, Nevoga Arena, Available at: http://www.hcorli.cz/zobraz.asp?t=stadion (Accessed: March 14, 2017).

Kacetl, Jiří (August 15, 2017) Introduction to Znojmo (translated from Czech to English),Available at: http://www.znojmocity.cz/vismo/dokumenty2.asp?id_org=19341&id=3021&n=uvodni-informace-o-znojme&p1=62877 (Accessed: March14, 2017).

Peroutka, Lukáš (August 6, 2016) Introducing Orli Znojmo: The Czech team proving itself in the international EBEL, Available at: http://www.championshockeyleague.com/en/chl-news/introducing-orli-znojmo-the-czech-team-proving-itself-in-theinternational-ebel(Accessed: September 17, 2016).

Radio Prague (February 13, 2016) Čížov - the last fragment of the Iron Curtain, Available at: http://www.czech.cz/en/Tourisme/Cizov-the-last-fragment-of-the-Iron-Curtain

(Accessed: March 10, 2017).

Správa Národního parku Podyjí, A Visit to Podyjí, Available at: http://www.nppodyji.cz/a-visit-to-podyji?lang=2 (Accessed: March 20, 2017).

The Editors of Encyclopaedia Britannica (July 19, 2017) Iron Curtain, Available at:https://www.britannica.com/event/Iron-Curtain (Accessed: August 1, 2017).

The Editors of Encyclopaedia Britannica (October 12, 2012) Znojmo, Available at:https://www.britannica.com/place/Znojmo (Accessed: March 30, 2017).

ZnojemskaBeseda.cz (August 29, 2017) History , Available at: http://www.znojemskabeseda.cz/underground/history/ (Accessed: August 29, 2017).

Znojemská beseda, History of the grape harvest , Available at: http://www.znojemskevinobrani.cz/history/ (Accessed: March 20, 2017).

Jesenice, Slovakia
Allcock, John B. (March 27, 2017) Yugoslavia, Available at: https://www.britannica.com/place/Yugoslavia-former-federated nation-1929-2003 (Accessed:March 28, 2017).

Burton, Tara Isabella (November 9, 2015) The lake at the end of the world, Available at:http://www.bbc.com/travel/story/20151031-the-lake-at-the-end-of-the-world (Accessed: April 13, 2017).

EliteProspects.com, HDD Jesenice, Available at: http://www.eliteprospects.com/team.php?team=15803 (Accessed: April 10, 2017).

EliteProspects.com, HK Jesenice, Available at: http://www.elite-prospects.com/team.php?team=819 (Accessed: April 10, 2017).

Gosar, Anton, Karl Lavrencic and Others (March 27, 2017) Slovenia, Available at:https://www.britannica.com/place/Slovenia (Accessed: March 28, 2017).

Hofmann, Paul (May 11, 1997) Savoring three cultures, Available at: http://www.nytimes.com/1997/05/11/travel/savoring-three-cultures.html?pagewanted=all (Accessed: April 13, 2017).

IIHF.com (March 24, 2009) Acroni defends title, Available at: http://www.iihf.com/home-of-12,ttnews%5Btnews%5D=7176&-cHash=5

Institute of Sport Jesenice (August 28, 2017) Športna dvorana Podmežakla - II. faza (translated from Slovenian to English), Available at: http://www.zsport-jesenice.si/info.php?id=razp&x=2014033 (Accessed: August 30, 2017).

Knific, B. (June 27, 2016) Chronology of the War for Slovenia - First Day (June 27, 1991)(translated from Slovenian to English), Available at: http://www.obramba.com/novice/kopno/kronologija-vojne-za-slovenijo-prvi-dan-27-junij-1991/ (Accessed: April 12, 2017).

Merk, Martin (July 9, 2012) Dark clouds overJesenice, Available at: http://www.iihf.com/home-ofhockey/news/news-singleview/?tx_ttnews%5Btt_news%5D=7074&cHash=4adfcf7e-51b01e9a814bf35a97fb7155 (Accessed: April 10, 2017).

Merk, Martin (September 3, 2012) The end of Acroni Jesenice, Available at: http://www.iihf.com/home-of-hockey/news/news-singleview/?tx_ttnews%5Bttnews%5D=7176&cHash=588b93af-167400f602ef13b612081530 (Accessed: April 10, 2017).

Slovenian cities and municipalities, Jesenice, Available at: http://mesta.slo-link.si/mesta/jesenice.html (Accessed: April 12, 2017).

Miskolc, Hungary
DVTK.eu (January 13, 2017) The retaining force of DVTK (translated from Hungarian to English), Available at: http://dvtk.eu/12461-A_DVTK_megtarto_ereje-cikk (Accessed: February 4, 2017).

DVTK.eu (July 27, 2016) "Whoever does not appreciate the past does not deserve the future" (translated from Hungarian to English), Available at: http://dvtk.eu/11421-Aki_a_multat_nem_becsuli_a_jovot_nem_erdemli-cikk (Accessed: April 4, 2017).

EliteProspects.com, DTVK Jegesmedvek , Available at: http://www.eliteprospects.com/team.php?team=3984 (Accessed: April 2, 2017).

EliteProspects.com, HC Nove Zamky, Available at: http://www.eliteprospects.com/team.php?team=2207 (Accessed: April 2, 2017).

Loonen, Joeri (March 26, 2013) Road Warriors, Available at: http://www.iihf.com/home-of-hockey/news/news-singleview/?tx_ttnews%5Btt_news%5D=7622&cHash=90af0a-519f5107674ad7d60d670c654f

(Accessed: April 4, 2017).

Miskolc.hu, Chronology – from the Seleta culture to the 20th century, Available at: http://miskolc.hu/en/culture/local-history/chronology-%E2%80%93-seleta-culture-20thcentury (Accessed: April 2, 2017).

The Editors of Encyclopaedia Britannica (September 15, 2010) Miskolc, Available at: https://www.britannica.com/place/Miskolc (Accessed: March 29, 2017).

Zavodszky, Szabolcs (March 22, 2016) Miskolc defends MOL title, Available at: http://www.iihf.com/home-of-hockey/news/news-singleview/?tx_ttnews%5Btt_news%5D=10483&cHash=360bcaf1417ddacf55a9d82355c59434 (Accessed: February 4, 2017).

Zavodszky, Szabolcs (March 24, 2017) DVTK Jegesmedvek on top, Available at: http://www.iihf.com/home-of-hockey/news/news-singleview/?tx_ttnews%5Btt_news%5D=11496&cHash=e04798638570418898d4de282ad43db1 (Accessed: March 27, 2017).

Zavodszky, Szabolcs (September 11, 2015) MOL League kicks off eighth season, Available at: http://www.iihf.com/home-of-hockey/news/news-singleview/?tx_ttnews%5Btt_news%5D=10002&cHash=103497490035d8377ddecd974cf66af2 (Accessed:February 4, 2017).

Prague, Czech Republic
Asiedu, Dita (April 5, 2005) World's biggest Stalin monument would have turned 50 on may day, Available at: http://www.radio.cz/en/section/curraffrs/worlds-biggest-stalin-monument-would-have-turned-50-on-may-day (Accessed: April 5, 2017).

Champions Hockey League (Decemeber 19, 2016) Road to final four: Sparta Prague, Available at: http://www.championshockey-league.com/en/chl-news/road-to-the-final-four-spartaprague (Accessed: March 29, 2017).

EliteProspects.com, HC Sparta Praha, Available at: http://www.eliteprospects.com/team.php?team=164&teamhistory=complete (Accessed: April 7, 2017).

HCSparta.cz, History (translated from Czech to English), Available at: http://www.hcsparta.cz/zobraz.asp?t=historie(Accessed: March 27, 2017).

HCSparta.cz, Klub Legend, Available at: http://legendy.hcsparta.cz/legendy.php (Accessed: March 14, 2017).

HCSparta.cz (April 2017) Historie, Available at: http://historie.hcsparta.cz/ (Accessed: March 28, 2017).

IIHF.com (2008) Story #18: Two games Czechoslovakia simply couldn't lose, Available at: http://www.iihf.com/iihf-home/the-iihf/100-year-anniversary/100-top-stories/story-18/ (Accessed: April 17, 2017).

IIHF.com (2008) Story #22: Bondra's Bomb - The biggest thing for Slovakia since independence , Available at: http://www.iihf.com/iihf-home/the-iihf/100-year-anniversary/100-topstories/story-22/ (Accessed: April 17, 2017).

IIHF.com (2008) Story #42: Breakup of old Europe creates a new hockey world, Available at: http://www.iihf.com/iihf-home/the-iihf/100-year-anniversary/100-top-stories/story-42/ (Accessed: April 17, 2017).

IIHF.com (2008) Story #48: Czechoslovakian team jailed for treason, entire generation lost, Available at: http://www.iihf.com/iihf-home/the-iihf/100-year-anniversary/100-top-stories/story-48/ (Accessed: April 19, 2017).

Lapointe, Joe (May 15, 1992) Hockey; Jagr's edge is tied to history, Available at: http://www.nytimes.com/1992/05/15/sports/hockey-jagr-s-edge-is-tied-to-history.html (Accessed: April 17, 2017).

Loonen, Joeri (January 1, 2013) The battle of Prague, Available at: http://www.iihf.com/home-ofhockey/news/news-singleview/?tx_ttnews%5Btt_news%5D=7517cHash=3548415740455f7e08f-f95a9364b8a8d(Accessed: April 2, 2017).

O'Brien, Derek (February 4, 2017) Sparta Prague: a long standing presence in international club hockey, Available at: http://www.championshockeyleague.com/en/chl-news/sparta-prague-alongstanding-presence-in-international-club-hockey (Accessed: August 16, 2017).

Osborne, Richard Horsely, Francis William Carter and Others (February 4, 2015) Prague, Available at: https://global.britannica.com/place/Prague (Accessed: April 16, 2017).

Sparta.cz, History AC Sparta Praha, Available at: http://www.sparta.cz/en/club/history/ac-spartapraha.shtml (Accessed: March 28, 2017).

Stavnice.cz, History (translated from Czech to English), Available at: http://www.stvanice.cz/historie.htm (Accessed: April 18, 2017).

The Canadian Press (September 29, 2011) Anisimov, Fedotenko lead Rangers to 2-0 win over Sparta Prague in Europe, Available at: http://www.thehockeynews.com/news/article/anisimovfedotenko-lead-rangers-to-2-0-win-over-sparta-prague-in-europe (Accessed: April 16, 2017).

The Editors of Encyclopaedia Britannica (July 22, 2011) Charles University, Available at: https://global.britannica.com/topic/Charles-University (Accessed: April 16, 2017).

The Editors of Encyclopaedia Britannica (March 27, 2017) Thirty Years War, Available at: https://www.britannica.com/event/Thirty-Years-War (Accessed: March 27, 2017).

The Editors of Encyclopaedia Britannica (March 28, 2017) Czechoslovakia, Available at: https://www.britannica.com/place/Czechoslovakia (Accessed: March 28, 2017).

The Editors of Encyclopaedia Britannica (October 26, 2016) Prague Spring, Available at: https://global.britannica.com/event/Prague-Spring (Accessed: April 16, 2017).

TipSportareana-Praha.cz, Arena, Available at: http://www.tipsportarena-praha.cz/arena/?lang=cs (Accessed: March 29, 2017).

USAHockey.com, 1992 IIHF Men's World Championship, Available at: http://teamusa.usahockey.com/page/show/2668970-1992-iihf-men-s-world-championship (Accessed: April 17, 2017).

Velikovská, Tereza and Marek Kratochvíl (July 14, 2014) Introducing Sparta Prague: over a century of tradition, Available at: http://www.championshockeyleague.com/en/chl-news/ introducing-sparta-prague-over-a-century-of-tradition (Accessed: April 2, 2017).

Dedicated to Amanda.
Thank you for the camera and encouragement.

www.ingramcontent.com/pod-product-compliance
Lightning Source LLC
Chambersburg PA
CBHW042015080426
42735CB00002B/56